'The late Clubman and the early Covent Garden Carman meet', run the subtitle to this illustration, which appeared in 'The Sphere' of 20th July 1901. Some provincial towns had a higher cab tariff at night, but not London. The picture captures well the rather rakish image of the hansom cab.

Victorian and Edwardian Horse Cabs

Trevor May

Shire Publications

Contents

Cover: *Cabs in The Strand, London in the 1890s. In the foreground is a 'Growler'; a Hansom cab, with its doors open, is behind it to the right. (NetXPosure.net)*

ACKNOWLEDGEMENTS

Illustrations are acknowledged as follows: author's collection, pages 1, 3 (both), 4 (top two), 5 (both), 6 (both), 7, 8, 9 (both), 11 (bottom), 12 (bottom), 13 (both), 14 (top left and bottom), 15 (all), 16 (middle two and bottom), 17 (top and centre right), 18 (both), 19 (bottom), 20 (both), 22 (both), 23 (all), 25 (top, centre left and bottom), 27, 28 (top), 29 (top and bottom), 30 (all), 31 (both), 32 (both); author's photograph, page 28 (bottom); Birmingham Public Library, page 26 (top); Bourne Hall Museum, page 16 (top); Dover Pictorial Archive, pages 4 (bottom), 12 (top), 14 (top right), 26 (bottom), 29 (centre); Hull Transport Museum, page 24 (both); Leicester Museums, page 25 (centre right); Metropolitan Police Museum, page 19 (top); Public Record Office, page 21.

British Library Cataloguing in Publication Data: May, Trevor. Victorian and Edwardian horse cabs. – (Shire album; no. 346) 1. Horse-drawn omnibuses – Great Britain – History – 19th century 2. Horse-drawn omnibuses – Great Britain – History – 20th century 3. Cab and omnibus service – Great Britain – History – 19th century 4. Cab and omnibus service – Great Britain – History – 20th century I. Title 629.2'2232'0941'09034 ISBN 0 7478 0430 3

Published in 2009 by Shire Publications Ltd, Midland House, West Way, Botley, Oxford OX2 0PH.
(Website www.shirebooks.co.uk)
Copyright © 1999 by Trevor May. First published 1999. Reprinted in 2009. Shire Library 346.
ISBN 978 0 7478 0430 3.

Printed in Great Britain by Ashford Colour Press Ltd, Unit 600, Fareham Reach, Fareham Road, Gosport, Hampshire PO13 0FW.

'Here I am, my good masters.' A hackney coachman with his coach, which, judging from the armorial bearings on the panels, started out as a gentleman's carriage – a common occurrence.

Before the horse cab

Until the nineteenth century most people walked to work and went about their business on foot. In London at the beginning of the Victorian era some 175,000 people crossed the Thames each day by London Bridge and Blackfriars Bridge alone, while the river remained what it had always been – the most important thoroughfare through the capital. The streets were filthy and congested. In 1853, visitors were advised in a German travel book to 'push forward without any false modesty, [for Londoners] give and receive kicks and pushes with . . . equanimity'.

Hackney coaches (public carriages for hire) began to appear in significant numbers in the 1620s, and in 1634 the first street stand was introduced. So great became their number ('caterpillar swarms of hirelings' was one caustic description) that hackney coaches were soon subject to regulation. In 1694 a body of Hackney Coach Commissioners was established for London. The Commissioners derived their authority from the Treasury, and they remained responsible for public carriages until 1832, the task eventually passing to the Metropolitan Police in 1850.

Although the number of hackney

A hackney coachman and a cad. It was the job of the waterman or 'cad' (shown left) to attend to the needs of hackneymen and their horses at the stands.

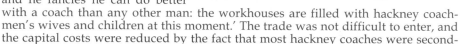

coaches was limited by law, it does not seem to have represented a serious monopoly, for there was a rapid turnover of licences. As one of the Commissioners commented in 1830, 'A gentleman's servant saves up two or £300 and marries and he fancies he can do better with a coach than any other man: the workhouses are filled with hackney coachmen's wives and children at this moment.' The trade was not difficult to enter, and the capital costs were reduced by the fact that most hackney coaches were second-hand gentlemen's coaches. They received only a cursory inspection as to fitness, which comes as no surprise when one learns that the four inspectors in 1830 (responsible for over a thousand vehicles) had previously been employed as a butler, a valet, a gardener and a land agent. In the following year, *The Times* expressed the view that: 'There is certainly in no town in Great Britain, or on the continent, so dirty and rickety a vehicle as a London hackney coach.'

> NEAT
> # HACKNEY COACHES,
> ### CABS, &c.
>
> RESIDENCES, { JOHN GERMAINE, *Great George Street* ; JACOB WOOD, *Merrion Street.*

Above: *The trade card of a Leeds hackneyman, c.1840. As well as operating cabs, hackney coaches and omnibuses, John Germaine also ran a beerhouse. There were around a dozen or more hackneymen in Leeds at this time.*

Right: *A Parisian fiacre, the name of which derives from the Irish St Fiacrius. It was outside the Hôtel de St Fiacre that the first hackney carriages stood waiting in the early seventeenth century. The term 'hackney' comes from the French word 'haquenée', used to describe an ambling nag.*

It was from Paris that the idea of horse cabs was introduced into Britain. This engraving of 1815 shows the 'cabriola' or 'cabriolet' then in use in the French capital.

The first horse cabs

Cabs were lighter vehicles drawn by one horse rather than the two to be found in the hackney coach. Their introduction had been authorised in 1815, but none was brought on to the London streets until 1823. Most hackneymen were small operators with little financial leeway, which made investment in untried vehicles risky and uninviting. The first cab operators were therefore gentlemen, more used to speculating in risky trading ventures. The two pioneers, J. H. Bradshaw and Benjamin Rotch, were respectively a banker and a barrister, the latter from a family with extensive British and American whaling interests. Others included a wine and spirit dealer, army officers, and an Ulster merchant with wide trading interests in South America and Mexico. That such men were involved indicates the extent of the trading opportunity which they discerned, but any hope of a profit was dependent on their control of the small number of licences which the Treasury was prepared to allow. There was a brisk competition for licences (although not from the conservative hackneymen) and their allocation afforded an additional means by which ministers might reward their friends.

With a pocketful of licences, the early proprietors intended to offer the public

George Shillibeer is best known as the originator of the London omnibus, but he also tried to secure cab licences in the dying days of the monopoly. He received the support of Hackney Coach Commissioner Edward Jesse, who wrote to the Treasury in 1831: 'I know little of Mr Shillibeer except that the public are much indebted to him for a new and useful description of carriage and he is, I think, one of those persons who ought to receive every encouragement.' He received very little, however, and lacked the business acumen to profit from the small number of cabs licensed to him.

An early side-seat cab viewed, untypically, from the rear. The licence plate appears to be attached to the hood.

a superior class of vehicle and driver, coupled with much more rapid transit. Speed was the thing. In *The Traveller's Oracle*, published in 1827, John Jervis regarded cabs as 'frightfully dangerous vehicles for town work', and he felt that they would 'only be used by those who are rash enough to sacrifice safety for celerity and comfort for cheapness'.

If the gentlemen were to make a profit they had to make it quickly, for in the 1820s the tide was beginning to run against monopolies. The Hackney Coach Commissioners were abolished at the beginning of 1832, and a year later the trade was thrown open, with no limit to the number of either coaches or cabs allowed on the streets. The gentlemen pulled out, and as they did so the hackneymen moved in. Within about a year cabs exceeded coaches in number, and by 1845, when the number of cabs had risen to 2500, fewer than two hundred hackney coaches remained.

As cabs became more popular in the 1830s, the search began for a suitable two-wheeled vehicle for public use. The cab (or cabriolet, to give it its full name) had been introduced from France in about 1810 and soon became a favoured vehicle for

An early side-seat cab. There could hardly be a sharper contrast between the naturalistic and elegant rendering of the passenger and the coarse caricature of the driver. However, this captures the attitude of many in the nineteenth century who considered cabmen to be of a different race or species.

The second series of Charles Dickens's 'Sketches by Boz' contained this engraving of a 'coffin cab' by George Cruikshank. The derivation of the name is self-evident. It will be noted that, for privacy or in the event of bad weather, the single passenger was able to draw a curtain across the front of his box.

'men about town'. They were fitted with a folding hood that gave a considerable measure of protection when raised. When not needed it was generally left 'set back' or 'half struck' rather than fully retracted, in order to afford room behind for a diminutive groom, or 'tiger', without whom no smart turnout was complete. Requirements were different for a public vehicle. There was no need for a groom, but it was necessary to make room for a driver, and physically to separate him from his passengers. This was done by widening the wheelbase and fitting in a tiny seat alongside the passenger compartment, but outside it. It was also necessary to construct the vehicles in a more robust manner, bearing in mind the speed with which they were worked and the rough usage that they received. The early cabs soon acquired a reputation for recklessness, enhanced by the publicity given to accidents, such as the death of Lady Caroline Barham, knocked down and killed by a fifteen-year-old driver in October 1832. The 'coffin cab' sounds a suitable title for such an apparently dangerous vehicle, but the reference was to a variant of the hooded cab, where the passenger compartment was replaced by a rigid, roofed compartment, perhaps best known from George Cruikshank's illustration for Dickens's *Sketches by Boz*.

The origins of the hansom cab

It was not until the mid 1830s that the hansom cab and four-wheeled 'growler' appeared, setting the standard for horse cabs that persisted right down to the introduction of the motor taxi. It is usually the hansom that we picture in our minds when we think of horse cabs, for that vehicle, clattering through swirls of fog, has become almost a symbol of Victorian London. Sherlock Holmes would have been powerless without it, and in 1891, the year that he first appeared in print, two-thirds of London's cabs were hansoms. They were also prominent, though not so dominant, in the provinces. In 1880, Manchester had a hundred hansoms, but 361 four-wheelers; while Newcastle still retained nearly as many two-horse cabs as single-horse ones. In smaller towns and seaside resorts it was often a different type of cab that prevailed, namely the victoria or fly, a four-wheeled carriage with a low, sweeping, cabriolet-like body. London cabs were not always thought the best. Henry Cole, one of the masterminds behind the Great Exhibition, wrote in 1867 that, from personal experience, 'cabs were better in Birmingham and Liverpool, and very much better in Edinburgh.'

That the hansom takes its name from Joseph Aloysius Hansom, architect of the Birmingham Town Hall and founder of *The Builder*, is well known. Less well known is the part played by John Chapman, a former clockmaker and manufacturer of lace-making machinery, who became an authority on Indian financial administration and a pioneer of aeronautics.

Hansom was only twenty-eight when, in 1831, he won the competition to design the Birmingham Town Hall, and the commission made his name. It also brought about his bankruptcy. As a condition of his contract with the Birmingham town commissioners, he had rashly entered into a bond on behalf of the builders, and when they ran into financial difficulties so did he. This may have been the spur that turned his attention to cabs, for his involvement in hackney carriages has never been satisfactorily explained. He needed to make money fast, and it was not long since

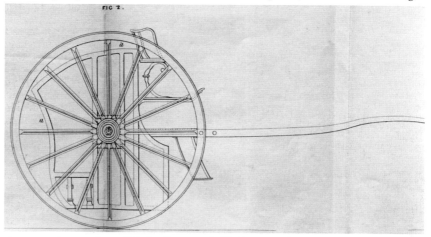

The hansom cab as we know it is hardly recognisable from Joseph Hansom's patent specification of 1834. The body – likened by some observers to a giant packing chest – was suspended on stub axles from wheels that were 7 feet (2.13 metres) in diameter. In addition, the vehicle was driven from the front. John Chapman was called in to remedy the major defects of the design and it was he, rather than Hansom, who came up with the hansom cab that we all know.

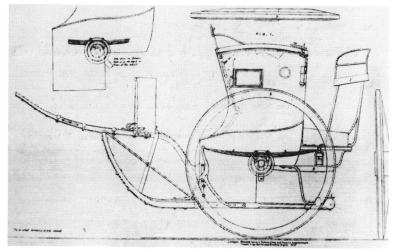

Side view of Chapman's improved cab, as illustrated in the patent that he took out with W. S. Gillett in 1836. The heavy undercarriage added so much to the weight that it was soon reduced to a rear skid. After a while, as the fear of accidents abated, these too were abandoned.

the exploits of the gentleman adventurers (their success greatly exaggerated) had been a matter of public debate. Other thoughts may have led him in that direction, for the patent that he took out in 1834 contained drawings and descriptions of *three* vehicles, 'for the conveyance of various kinds of loads on common and other roads'. One was the prototype 'hansom' cab; a second was an ingenious (but totally impractical) vehicle, in which spoked wheels were replaced by two giant hoops, revolving between rollers – the idea being that entrance to the vehicle could be obtained *through* the wheels; the third was a device for carrying heavy blocks of stone. The likelihood in that Hansom's work on the Birmingham Town Hall had him to the idea of this last vehicle first, for part of the financial difficulty of the builders had arisen from the high cost of transporting marble from Anglesey before the coming of the railway. If that is the case, he must have quickly perceived that his ideas were transferable to other types of vehicle including public cabs, which were still passing through a developmental stage.

Hansom's experimental cab was a cumbersome affair. Nevertheless, backed by a group of Warwickshire and Leicestershire businessmen, Hansom had a prototype built by John Fullylove, a Hinckley coachbuilder, and it was driven up to London.

A Chapman-style hansom cab, from the 'Illustrated London News' in 1844. These early hansoms were heavier than later types and lacked their elegant lines. The early types can be distinguished by the sledge-like undercarriage, which was intended to give security to passengers in the event of a broken shaft or wheel.

Cutting a dash! A railway promoter races to the Board of Trade to get his plans in before a deadline. This picture, from the 'Illustrated London News' of 6th December 1845, captures well the spirit of the early Victorian hansom. Even so, the vehicle looks heavier than later types, as indeed it was; but this appearance is accentuated by the way in which the body sits lower over the axle.

Financial difficulties also beset Chapman, his machinery business ruined by trade depression and difficulties with the Customs and Excise department. With a pregnant wife to support, he too headed for London. He tramped round the engineering workshops looking for employment and before long had secured an introduction to Hansom and his partners, who had taken premises near Regent's Park.

Hansom seems quickly to have tired of his invention. He had turned to other things in Hinckley, and he was content to leave Chapman to develop the cab, a task to which the latter turned an engineer's eye. Initially he replaced the body with one resembling more closely that with which we are familiar, although at first he retained the front driving position shown in the patent. The Safety Cabriolet and Two-wheel Carriage Company was set up early in 1836, and five cabs were put on the streets – the forerunners, it was hoped, of a much larger fleet – and about fifty bodies were ordered. This proved to be a costly commercial blunder, however, for problems quickly arose. The framework of the cab (which alone weighed 4 hundredweight or 202 kg) was unsprung, and the horse was struck whenever the carriage ran over an obstacle. Sometimes the weight was thrown suddenly on the horse's back; sometimes the force was upwards, upon the belly-band. The poor animal, said Chapman, 'was so beaten upwards, downwards and sideways, that he was very quickly worn out.' The design placed strain upon the horse, the vehicle *and* the passenger, who was obliged to squeeze between the safety frame and the large, often muddy wheels in order to get in or out.

Chapman decided to return to first principles. The vehicle must be made to balance, whether empty or with a passenger. This could be achieved, he calculated, by placing the driver *behind* the vehicle. In 1836, Chapman, together with W. S. Gillett, a large shareholder in the company, took out a new patent. The directors, with some justification, complained of a conflict of interest, but there was little they could do. Legal opinion suggested that Hansom's patent was badly drafted and would not hold up in a court of law. Chapman had now come up with a better vehicle and a stronger patent. They had little choice but to enter into a licensing agreement with him.

In 1838 the company was renamed the Patent Safety Cab Company, and it was the largest cab concern in London. It also survived longer than most, not going out of business until the mid 1850s. But it did not make a fortune, for pirate cabs appeared in increasing numbers, and the patent rights proved impossible to protect. No more fortunate were Hansom and Chapman, and they turned to other things. One consequence of those fifty old bodies was that they had 'Hansom's Patent' painted on them, even though Chapman had done much of the work. That name stuck in the public's mind, so a 'hansom' it became, and not a 'chapman', which might have been more just.

The four-wheeled 'growler'

Some four-wheeled cabs appear to have been in use in the 1820s, but the 'classic' four-wheeler – based on the private clarence and brougham carriages – dates from about the same time as the introduction of the hansom. The four-wheeler was the maid-of-all-work of the hackney carriage trade and had a reputation to match. The coachbuilder G. N. Hooper wrote in the 1880s that:

These vehicles cannot be compared with the hansoms for style, comfort and finish. A large proportion of them are still coarse, noisy, odoriferous, and jumpy as regards the springs. When, however, it is considered to what uses they are put, some excuse may be offered for their shortcomings. For they take Jack and his mate on their arrival from Sheerness or Portsmouth; Tommy Atkins and his friends, perhaps fresh from camp life at Aldershot or Colchester; or Mary Jane and her boxes to her new place in a distant suburb; and as it is often cheaper to hire a cab than a cart to remove goods (other than personal luggage), it is hardly to be wondered at that the varnish is not as brilliant as on the duke's brougham or the countess's victoria.

It was for good reason that the four-wheeled cab became known as a 'growler', while Disraeli dubbed the hansom 'the gondola of London'.

In this cartoon from 'Punch' in 1863, the caption reads: Old Lady, 'But, going in four wheel cabs! I'm so afraid of small pox.' Cabby, 'You've no call to be afraid of my cab, Mum, for I've 'ad the hind wheel waccinated, and it took beautiful!' The fear was not groundless, for, until prevented by law later in the century, cabs (growlers especially) were frequently used as makeshift ambulances and often carried patients with infectious diseases.

Everything but the kitchen sink – but including the bath! A Euston station privileged growler piled high with luggage. The rail at the back of the cab, used to secure luggage more firmly, was known in the trade as a 'toolittle', having been introduced by one Tommy Toolittle. Hansoms could not compete with four-wheeled cabs in carrying capacity, with the result that growlers did much of the station work. In cities with more than one railway terminus, transfer work provided much employment for cabs.

Both in London and the provinces, much of the work done by four-wheelers was connected with the railway, for hansoms could compete with neither the amount of luggage nor the number of passengers carried. Most railway companies jealously guarded access to their stations, with the consequence that from their very inception they limited the number of cabs that had the right to ply for hire there. This they did by granting to selected cab operators (for an agreed sum of money) what was known as 'the privilege'. Any cab could drop passengers off, for the companies were not going to turn them away; but only privileged cabs were allowed to use the station cab stand in order to pick up passengers. If there were not enough cabs to meet any particular demand, then station staff would call in outside cabs, known in the trade as 'bluchers' for, like the eponymous field marshal at Waterloo, they were 'last on the field'. The railway companies defended the privilege on the grounds that it secured them a better class of cab and allowed them greater control over the drivers, but each of these assertions (the former, especially) was hotly contested. It

was argued that privileged proprietors did not send their best cabs to the stations, because they got knocked about so much by luggage. One large proprietor in London estimated that the maintenance of his privileged cabs cost 12.5 per cent more than that of his street cabs. There were also critics who alleged that the dark interiors of stations, with passengers eager to be on their way after perhaps a long rail journey, were ideal places to send cabs and horses not of the best quality. It is difficult to get to the truth, and the issue remained one which poisoned relations in the trade until it was abolished in 1907.

A privileged cab of the South Eastern Railway at Charing Cross. Lithograph from the 'Illustrated London News', 19th April 1890. In May 1883 the South Eastern Railway abandoned the privilege, on an experimental basis, at its three termini of Charing Cross, London Bridge and Cannon Street. But, for reasons which are unclear (although there is a hint of 'dirty tricks' on the part of certain privileged proprietors), the experiment was not a success, and within four years had failed entirely. The Amalgamated Cab Drivers' Society, which had brokered the trial, took responsibility for guaranteeing £40 a week to the company, which it planned to recoup from the drivers at a rate of 1d per visit. The union defaulted; its secretary absconded; and in the subsequent turmoil the ACDS broke up. In February 1887 the South Eastern Railway reintroduced the privilege, although growing militancy on the part of the cab drivers kept the issue alive throughout the 1890s.

The men who ran the cabs

People who operated cabs often did so as part of some other equestrian business, such as that of livery-stable keeper, or jobmaster. The cabs that they ran were only one type of vehicle amongst many that they made available, others often including omnibuses and hearses or mourning coaches, as well as a variety of private carriages. Although the majority of establishments were small, some could be very large. One of the largest jobmasters was the London-based firm of Thomas Tilling. In 1892 it was claimed that Tilling supplied horses for the London Fire Brigade, the Salvage Corps and the Metropolitan Police. He had horses in the carts of a London district board of works, and another hundred in Peak Frean's biscuit vans. He supplied horses for tram companies and had horses out on job as far north as Sunderland and as far west as Cornwall. He also ran London omnibuses and cabs of his own. Out of 2026 London cab proprietors in 1861, he was by far the largest, possessing seventy-nine licences. At that time, 96 per cent of the London cab proprietors held no more than ten licences, while nearly 26 per cent owned only one.

The cab trade of the provinces tended to mirror that of the metropolis. In major urban centres such as Manchester, Birmingham and Glasgow, cabs served much the same purpose as in London. They met the needs of business and pleasure, and they serviced the railways. After the railway termini opened in Glasgow, the number of cabstands increased five-fold in two decades. In the mid 1860s, John Walker of Glasgow kept 366 horses and paid £500 a year for the privilege at Buchanan Street and Queen Street stations. In some towns, cabs served more specialised needs. Amongst such places were seaside resorts and watering places. There, holiday-makers, invalids and convalescents had to be attended to, and the authorities might find themselves having to license wheelchairmen as well as hackney men. Brighton, by 1890, had 1055 licensed cab drivers and 274 wheelchair drawers. They were well organised and in 1870 had formed the first branch of the Amalgamated Cab Drivers'

Left. Some indication of the scale of cab concerns can be gained from the advertisements for cab stock in 'The Times'. The advertisements shown here date from July 1853.

Below: *Much cab stock (both horses and carriages) was purchased by smaller proprietors second-hand, and there were auction houses that specialised in such things. One of the largest was Aldridge's in St Martin's Lane, London, shown here in an engraving from the 'Illustrated London News', 1883. At that time cabs could be purchased at stock sales at prices ranging from around 8 to 30 guineas or more, with second-hand Forders going for nearer 60 guineas. A decent cab horse would then have averaged around 35 guineas.*

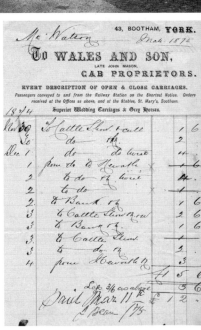

Left: *Many early nineteenth-century property developers, including the Bedford Estate in London, overestimated the demand for stable accommodation, and mews sometimes degenerated rapidly. Many cab yards were to be found in places such as Keppel Mews, pictured here in the 'Daily Graphic' in 1906, prior to their demolition for the building of Malet Street.*

Right: *John Thomson was a documentary photographer, whose 'Street Life in London' was published in 1877. The accompanying text gives details of this particular cabman, who had started life as a potboy in a public house, joined a tramway company as a conductor, and worked his way up to the position of timekeeper. After careful saving he took out a licence, purchased a horse, and hired a cab. Before too long he had earned enough to buy his own cab. Like this individual, the majority of cab proprietors were 'one-number men', large proprietors and cab companies being in the minority.*

Society outside London. The town had its own Cabmen's Mission and for a short while produced an evangelical Christian magazine, *The Cabmen's Messenger*.

Many cab drivers owned their own vehicle. Generally two horses were worked in rotation, but it was necessary to provide for replacements in case of sickness or injury. This meant that the owner of a single cab had to keep three horses if he were to enjoy any measure of security, but even then it was a risky business. The death of a horse or serious injury could quickly spell ruin.

If a proprietor owned more than one cab it would be necessary to employ additional drivers, and here there does appear to have been a difference between London and elsewhere. Outside London the driver was quite likely to be a paid employee, but within the metropolis he was a *bailee*, hiring the cab from the owner for a fixed sum per day, and hoping to exceed that sum in fares and tips. The rate varied according to the London Season, for there was a great diminution in trade when the upper classes moved back to their country seats. For this reason, the number of men employed as drivers varied greatly throughout the year. Part-time drivers were known in the trade

Like many cab proprietors, Wales & Son of York were jobmasters, letting out carriages on hire, either with or without drivers. This bill of March 1875 is for journeys principally to and from a cattle show. Exhibitions and attractions of any sort brought much work to cabmen.

ALFRED PARGETTER,
STONEY STANTON ROAD, COVENTRY.

HOUSEHOLD REMOVALS.
A. PARGETTER,
STONEY STANTON ROAD,
FOLESHILL, COVENTRY.

FURNITURE REMOV'ED to ALL PARTS
WITHOUT PACKING ESTIMATES FREE

Removal
Contractor
by Road
or
Rail.

Estimates
Furnished.

COMPLETE FUNERAL FURNISHER, &c.
HEARSES and FUNERAL COACHES to meet any Train,
by Wire, Post, or Telephone.

ORDERS PROMPTLY ATTENDED TO.

Telegrams:
"Pargetter,
S. S. Road,
Coventry."

Telephone
No. 343.

CABS,
BREAKS,
LANDAUS,
&c., &c.

Parties
Catered for.

Characteristically, the Coventry jobmaster Alfred Pargetter had his finger in a number of equine pies. As well as running cabs and having carriages for hire, he supplied mourning coaches and hearses and was also a removal contractor. Advertisement from 'Kelly's Warwickshire Directory' of 1900.

as 'butterflies', for they came out only when the weather was good. Although there were many men who devoted their lives to the trade, there were many others who saw cab driving as an occasional occupation that they could fit in with other casual employment.

All had to be licensed, but in London little attention was paid to a man's ability to drive, and it was not until 1896 that the Metropolitan Police introduced a driving test for horse-cabmen. This was thirty years after they had introduced the famous test of 'the knowledge'. Cab proprietors (who wanted a pool of surplus drivers in order to suppress pay) complained that the 'knowledge' test was too difficult. Established cab drivers, who saw it as a means of keeping out casuals, argued that it was too lax. It is hard to get at the truth; the test certainly became more structured as the years passed, and it probably became more difficult, although it never proved as demanding as the test faced by today's aspiring London taxi drivers.

The authorities seemed to be far more interested in a man's honesty for, ever since the days of the old hackney coaches, drivers of public carriages of all sorts were seen as men open to the gravest temptations. Since its formation in 1698, the Society for Promoting Christian Knowledge had provided specially written tracts for groups

METROPOLITAN
Drinking Fountain & Cattle Trough
ASSOCIATION.

Supported entirely by Voluntary Contributions.

OFFICES:
VICTORIA HOUSE, 111, VICTORIA STREET, WESTMINSTER, S.W.

President—His Grace the Duke of Westminster, K.G., etc., etc.
Chairman of Committee and Treasurer—Joseph Fry, Esq.
Secretary—M. W. Milton.

THIS IS THE ONLY SOCIETY FOR PROVIDING
Free Supplies of Water for Man and Beast in the Streets of London.

The relief which it affords both to human beings and dumb animals is incalculable.

If it had not been for the operations of this Society, thousands of people, young and old, who now quench their thirst at the Fountains, would probably be driven to the public-house, and if it were not for the Troughs, the amount of suffering amongst the multitude of dumb animals continually crowding round them would be inconceivable. Half-an-hour spent at one of them during the heat of the summer would do more to secure sympathy and support for the Association than any words which the Committee can use, they therefore very earnestly solicit liberal contributions, and trust the work will not be permitted to languish for want of funds.

Annual Subscriptions and Donations will be thankfully received by the Bankers, Messrs. Ransom, Bouverie, & Co.: Messrs. Barclay, Bevan, & Co.: or at the Office by

M. W. Milton, Secretary.

FORM OF BEQUEST.
"I give and bequeath the sum of ___ to be paid (free of Legacy Duty) out of such parts of my personal estate as can be lawfully applied for that purpose unto the Treasurer for the time being of a Society called or known by the name of The Metropolitan Drinking Fountain and Cattle Trough Association, to be at the disposal of the Committee for the time being of the said Society.

Left and below: The Metropolitan Drinking Fountain and Cattle Trough Association was founded in 1859. Although its advertisement showed a number of cab horses drinking from the street trough, many proprietors forbade their drivers from allowing the practice, which, they feared, carried the danger of picking up such contagious diseases as glanders, which could easily close down a stable. In time, the society extended its activities beyond the capital. The trough illustrated is to be found in Barrack Road, Exeter, where it was installed in 1917. Many cab yards kept a goat, which, for some strange reason, was thought to keep glanders at bay.

Prominent amongst these vehicles returning from the Derby at the turn of the twentieth century is a hansom cab. Derby Week started the high point of the London cabman's year, when the daily charge he had to pay for his cab rose to between 15s and 18s. On Derby Day itself, he might have to pay as much as 35s to 40s, so great were the chances of rich pickings. Then, after the Eton and Harrow Cricket Match, the price began to fall, until it reached a low point of around 11s between August and November.

Above left: 'Vel, it all'us wos so,' complains the cabman, 'the genteeler the Party, the wosser the Fare.' The preferred passenger of the cabman was the regular user, who knew the fares but was generous in tipping. Less regular passengers, including visitors from the country and many women, were less familiar with the etiquette of the relationship and were more nervous of being overcharged. The driver in such circumstances was more likely to get the exact fare and no more. From 'Punch', 1853.

Above right: Few cab drivers could look more sober and respectable than these; but all were nevertheless considered at moral risk and were prime targets for home missionaries. In this case, Mr Sunners of the Liverpool Town Mission has a handful of improving tracts to pass on. In the capital, the London City Mission made a massive effort to bring religion to cabmen and to improve their morals. Engraving from the 'British Workman', November 1859.

Left: Since 1715, hackney carriages in London paid a weekly duty, which stood at 10s in 1853. In that year it was reduced to 7s, but, partly as a concession to the Sunday Observance lobby, a new class of six-day cabs was introduced, with a reduced duty of 6s. Around a quarter of all cabs operated on this basis, and they were distinguished by licence plates of a different colour, numbered 10,000 upwards. This arrangement lasted until 1869, when the duties were abolished. Joseph Powell was one such six-day cabman. In this engraving from the 'British Workman' he is seen wrapped up in the traditional layered cape, and with a religious tract in his hands.

A dejected group of drivers wait in the rain to be hired. The boon of cabmen's shelters did not come until late in the nineteenth century, and even then many stands were without them. Illustration from the 'Leisure Hour', 1892.

CABMEN'S SHELTER FUND.
OFFICES—185, VICTORIA STREET, S.W.

President
HIS GRACE THE DUKE OF PORTLAND.

Hon. Treasurer.	Hon. Secretary.
CAPT. G. C. H. ARMSTRONG.	WALTER H. MACNAMARA, Esq.

THIS FUND was established in 1875 for the purpose of supplying Cabmen, when on the ranks, with a place of shelter where they can obtain good and wholesome refreshments at very moderate prices. The Shelters are supplied with papers and small Libraries are attached to many of them. No charge is made to the driver for admission.

Forty Shelters have now been placed in various parts of the Metropolis, and are used by over 3000 Cabmen daily.

The Committee desire to extend the movement, so that eventually every cab stand in the Metropolis of sufficient size may be provided with a place of shelter in inclement weather for those who at present are driven to the public-house for refreshment and warmth.

DONATIONS and ANNUAL SUBSCRIPTIONS in aid of this Fund will be thankfully received by the Honorary Secretary at the Office, or by the Bankers, Messrs. BARCLAY, BEVAN, TRITTON, RANSOM, BOUVERIE & Co., Pall Mall, S.W.

BRABAZON H. MORRIS, Gen. Superintendent.

FORM OF BEQUEST.

"I give and bequeath unto the Treasurer, for the time being, of the Charitable Institution known as the CABMEN'S SHELTER FUND, London, the sum of _____ pounds, to be paid, free of Legacy Duty, out of such part of my Personal Estate as I may by law bequeath to Charitable Institutions, to be applied towards the general purposes of the said Fund, and to be payable as soon after my decease as possible."

* The sum to be expressed in words, not figures.

Above: Thirteen years before the Cabmen's Shelter Fund started to bring cab shelters to London, this simple shelter was erected by public subscription in Upper Brook Street, Manchester. It opened in March 1862 and was built at a cost of £20, including furnishings. As with many such charitable efforts, this shelter was seen as a means of improving the morals of cabmen, for 'no games of chance, or cards, or dice are allowed in it, nor are any intoxicating drinks to be consumed, except at dinner or supper time.' Engraving from the 'Illustrated London News', 6th December 1862.

Right: Cab shelters were brought to London largely through the efforts of the Cabmen's Shelter Fund. At least a dozen surviving examples throughout Britain have become 'listed' buildings.

perceived to be in grave moral jeopardy, including soldiers and sailors, innkeepers – and hackneymen. This started a missionary zeal towards cabmen that has continued (through the work of the London City Mission) to this day.

Cab drivers were often depicted as rapacious creatures, preying on the innocent: whether foreigners, people up from the country, or that great Victorian favourite, 'the unprotected female'. Then, as now, they probably preferred regular users who understood the fare structure and were used to tipping. The cabman's earnings fluctuated a great deal, but one thing seems quite certain – that on the legal fares alone the driver would have had poor pickings. Nor were drivers always the offending party. A great grievance amongst them was the difficulty of gaining legal redress against 'bilking', or stealing away without paying the fare. Cabmen knew

A comparison of these two illustrations shows how little has changed since Victorian times. On the left is a modern photograph of the cab shelter at Warwick Avenue in west London, which was built in 1888 and is one of the earliest surviving examples in the capital. The right-hand picture, showing the interior of a cabmen's shelter, comes from the 'Illustrated London News', 1890. These drivers seem to have exhausted their legendary gift for repartee and are eating their meals in monastic silence. Many of the original shelters did not supply food but cooked the food that the men themselves brought in.

the likely places for a disappearing act to take place and would be nervous if asked to wait at any place where there was a multiplicity of entrances and exits. There was little that the driver could do. Before 1879 the offence was a criminal one (although it was almost impossible for the driver ever to press charges) but the Summary Jurisdiction Act of 1879 removed the criminal element and made the recovery of a fare a civil matter. Although the law was amended in 1896, the Act was badly drafted, and drivers continued to suffer.

Drivers received little sympathy. To many people they were a nuisance, although a necessary one. This was equally true when it came to cab stands. The ideal for most people was a cab stand in the next street – but not their own. Part of the problem originally was the lack of toilet and other facilities for drivers, who tended to loiter on pavements unless required, by order, to remain upon the box.

Like so many innovations in the cab trade, the idea of the cab shelter came from the provinces. Edinburgh had one in 1859, and ten years later Liverpool acquired its first one – a permanent, brick-built construction, costly to erect and obstructive to traffic. The solution of providing a removable, wooden structure was arrived at in Birmingham, where the first one was opened in 1872, outside the Town Hall, an unwitting tribute to Joseph Hansom. Within five years Birmingham had a dozen such shelters, and in 1875 the Cabmen's Shelter Fund was established, with the aim of providing a similar service in the metropolis.

Policing the cabs

London's cabs are unique in that, to this day, they remain the responsibility of central government. During the time of the Hackney Coach Commissioners, the responsible department was the Treasury. From 1838, the Home Office gradually gained control, and that department (working through the Metropolitan Police) remained in charge until 1984, when regulation of London's taxicabs passed to the Department of Transport.

The Metropolitan Police acquired its powers gradually and in a somewhat haphazard manner. In 1843, the Commissioner of Police was given the power to appoint cab stands, but he soon found that wherever he might propose to place one he was sure to be criticised. In 1851 the then Commissioner, Sir Richard Mayne, complained that 'The appointment of the Standings was the most obnoxious job I have ever had to get through.' Indeed, for a long time many officers refused to regard the supervision of public carriages as 'proper police work', and it was with no great enthusiasm that Mayne took over virtually complete control of the trade in 1850. From 1853 cabs had to

be inspected by the police and would only receive a licence if deemed to be in fit and proper condition. The hope that this would raise the standard of cab stock was frustrated by the ease with which proprietors could transfer a plate from a good cab (which had been sent for inspection) to an inferior

Approved! An illustration from 'Black and White', August 1891. The accompanying text points out: 'The ordeal of examining a cab is not severe. The official glances his eye over it, and produces a pot of yellow ochre, a shaving brush and a stencil plate, and on the body of the cab, on the back, he works a device of a crown, a wreath (with the month and the year in the centre), and underneath the word "Approved" and the initials of the Chief Commissioner, "E.R.C.B."

The original title of this engraving, which appeared in the 'Leisure Hour' in 1892, was 'The Reign of Law!'. In fact, the Metropolitan Police frequently complained of their limited powers to regulate street traffic. It was a grievance of cabmen that they suffered in consequence, as the powers possessed by the police over cabs were greater than those over private vehicles.

For most of the nineteenth century the authorities in London showed remarkably little interest in a man's ability to drive a cab. Not until 1896 was a driving test introduced for horse-cab drivers, who were examined in vehicles provided under contract by the great London jobmaster, Thomas Tilling. Illustration from George R. Sims, 'Living London', 1906.

Right: *In the provinces, cabs were regulated under local bylaws. In London, the Metropolitan Police Commissioner issued regulations. This poster (issued at some time between 1880 and 1890) warns of the seriousness of drunkenness and furious and careless driving. There is little evidence that cab drivers were more guilty of these offences than other drivers, but it was easier for the police to get at them.*

P.C.O. 44.

NOTICE.
PUBLIC CARRIAGES.

Many Serious Accidents, and, in some cases, Loss of Life, having resulted from Drunkenness and Furious or Careless Driving, The Commissioner of Police feels it his duty to warn Drivers of Hackney and Stage Carriages that a Conviction of either of the above Offences will be seriously considered, and may lead to a Refusal of the Licence.

J. MONRO,

The Commissioner of Police of the Metropolis.

Metropolitan Police Office,
Public Carriage Branch.

one. To combat this, a stencil later came to be used to mark the month and year of inspection, but inventive and unscrupulous proprietors even found a way of transferring this.

More significant than inspection, perhaps, was the power given to the Commissioner to lay down regulations for vehicle construction. In 1858, for example, cabs were required to have knobs and straps fitted to their windows, as well as iron frames on the roof for the better securing of luggage. By the 1870s, these requirements, which had originally been issued as separate orders, were codified into published *Notices to Proprietors as to Conditions for Obtaining a Certificate of Fitness.* These could be used to influence the design as well as the quality of cabs and were to be of crucial importance in determining the way in which motor cabs would develop.

Outside London, cabs were the responsibility of the local authority, but a measure of uniformity was introduced by the Town Police Clauses Act, 1847, which set out the parameters for bylaws. Until 1884 these had to be confirmed by the Home Secretary, who often passed them to the Commissioner of the Metropolitan Police for comment. After that date the confirmation of draft bylaws passed to the Local Government Board. It was open to the local authority to limit the number of cabs (a provision which some argued would have improved the cabs of London had it been applied there). Not many local authorities adopted such a measure. In 1894 only seven out of sixty-two authorities circularised by the Metropolitan Police were found to do so. Leeds was one that did: it then had 159 cabs (fifty of them hansoms) but the ratio of cabs to population was 1:2300, compared with 1:500 in London.

Harvey's New Curricle Tribus, from the 'Illustrated London News', 29th March 1845. Like many earlier cabs, the driver's seat is placed on the offside, rather than at the rear. Harvey's cab could take three passengers and might also be converted to single-horse draught. However, like most improved cabs, it never caught on.

Improved cabs

There were many attempts to improve upon the design of both two- and four-wheeled cabs, but their form remained fundamentally unchanged until a new standard for hansoms was set in the 1870s by Forder, a coachbuilding firm based in Wolverhampton. The problem with cabs was that they were anonymous. In a city such as London, the chances of coming across the same cab and driver a second time (unless a regular booking was made) were minimal. One cab was very much like another, and they charged the same fares. The difficulty for a proprietor who

Evans's and Felton's improved cabs were exhibited at the 1862 International Exhibition held in London. The principal feature of the former was the underspringing of the shafts. Felton's cab (bottom) is described as a brougham 'shofle'. 'Shofle' (or 'showfull') was the slang word used in the trade to refer to a hansom cab. It means counterfeit and was first applied to the cabs that infringed Hansom's patent.

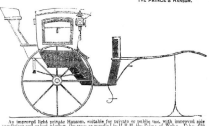
Left: *Jno. Marston & Co of Birmingham were amongst the principal manufacturers of hansom cabs. This advertisement of c.1883 shows the Imperial Brougham Hansom (top) and the Prince's Hansom (bottom). The Imperial Brougham should be compared with the illustration on page 24 of a bow-fronted brougham hansom (also by Marston) in the collection of Hull Transport Museum.*

FLOYD'S PATENT HANSOM CAB.

Above: *The Floyd Cab was designed in the early 1880s, and the Floyd Cab Company was floated in 1885 to promote it. It was not a commercial success. A forward hood (or calash), having front and side windows, could be made to fall in a curve from the roof of the cab. While this protected the passengers from bad weather, it added greatly to the weight. The few that were produced were often lavishly appointed and were adapted for private use.*

Joseph Parlour was the inventor of the 'Parlour four-seat hansom', first shown at the 1885 Inventions Exhibition, and developed by John Abbot of Bideford as the 'Devon' cab. The cab was designed to give ladies easier access, but it was not a commercial success.

A bow-fronted hansom cab of 1889, manufactured by Marston of Birmingham, operated by Richardson's of Hull, and currently in the collection of Hull Transport Museum. Richardson's, like many horse-cab firms, eventually moved into motor cabs and still operates in Hull.

expended capital on introducing innovative cabs was that he was generally prohibited from charging a higher fare to recoup his outlay, although (if he were an owner-driver) he might earn more in tips if he had a better-quality cab. An attempt by the authorities to encourage superior cabs by allowing proprietors to set and display their own fares was made in London in 1869, but it did not prove successful, and fixed fares were reintroduced two years later. On the whole, the public did not show much interest in new-fangled cabs and preferred to stick with the vehicles they knew. Responding to the appearance of an engraving of the New Patent Curricle Tribus in the *Illustrated London News*, a writer in *Punch* pointed out that:

> [Designs for improved cabs] appear in the *Illustrated News*, but are never carried out. They run through all the coffeehouses in the world inside its columns, and then, as if their journey was completed, they suddenly pull up, go home, and you never see anything more of them. They only come out to go in again. The poor things have their portraits taken, and then die.

A cab oddity. This three-wheeled cab, to be seen at the Hull Transport Museum, was built around 1900 and was designed to carry four passengers. The cranked rear axle helps to keep the body low. This feature, in addition to the angled front door, made access easier. It is not known whether this vehicle was licensed for public use.

Left: *The Forder cab was the only improved variety to win widespread acceptance and, by the end of the horse-cab era, it had swept the field. Advertisement from 'Kelly's Warwickshire Directory', 1900.*

Below: *Forder never secured a monopoly of improved cabs as speculators had hoped, for the patent was difficult to protect and many other builders copied the design. This cab is one such example. Built by Roake of London, it is now in the collections of Leicester Museums.*

Left: *Sir James Dugdale Astley was typical of the 'sporting' gentlemen who took to running cabs in the 1880s. Nicknamed 'the Mate', he was an athlete as well as a great racing man. Astley gave his driver 25s a week in standing wages. When not needing the cab himself, Astley let it ply for hire and took 10s a day from the driver. He claimed that, 'with three nags, I could work both cabs well, and my riding cost me comparatively little.' His 'nags' were his less successful racehorses. At least one horse continued in its former ways - in 1884 it bolted down Piccadilly and knocked over a vanman, seriously injuring him. Astley had to pay £125 in damages and promptly gave up the cab trade.*

Left: *The London Improved Cab Company was the most successful of a number of cab companies formed in the 1880s, and by 1894 it was operating nearly three hundred cabs. A huge depot was maintained off Gray's Inn Road, with shoeing forges and repair shops, and there was a model stable in Chelsea (shown here). This three-storey building was built in a square, with standing room for cabs on the ground floor and stables on the first and second. Illustration from 'Black and White', 1891.*

The Birmingham Cab Company had a tempestuous history between its registration in 1885 and its dissolution in 1891, during which time it unsuccessfully tried to gain a monopoly of cab operation in that city. This cartoon, which appeared locally at a time when the directors were facing financial investigation in 1887, is of interest because of the vehicle it shows. This is a patent 'Victoria-Hansom', which could be converted from a closed hansom to an open, two-wheeled victoria. The idea was an interesting one, but the public did not take to it.

ELEVENTH Year. No. 552. THE DART. Friday, May 20th. 1887

"WHERE?"

However, a vehicle that did not serve as a public vehicle might very well serve as a *private* one. Many wealthy and professional men who made great use of cabs purchased their own, and a vehicle of better quality or unusual design might well meet their requirements.

Some entrepreneurs (especially if they controlled patent rights) saw a commercial opportunity in starting up fleets of improved cabs, hoping that large numbers would make them visible in the streets. Few were successful. The Shrewsbury and Talbot **ST** Cab and Noiseless Tyre Company was one that was. Started by the twentieth Earl of Shrewsbury (whose seat, Alton Towers, is a modern capitalist success story), it came up with the winning combination of fitting rubber tyres to Forder cabs. There was a double advantage. Rubber tyres made wheels last three times as long, and they gave the public a more comfortable ride. However, even Shrewsbury's cab company lacked overall success, the profitable side being the licensing of patented rubber tyres to other users.

Hansom cabs were unique neither to London nor even to Britain. Fergus Hume's best-selling crime novel of 1886, 'The Mystery of a Hansom Cab', was set in Melbourne, Australia. Hansoms were familiar in a number of American cities. The smart turnout shown here comes from the 1893 catalogue of C. M. Moseman & Brother of New York, who were amongst the most prominent suppliers of harness and other equestrian goods. Forder exported cabs to America, their private clients including the millionaires Andrew Carnegie and William K. Vanderbilt. The chairman of Forder claimed that many American tourists purchased hansoms in London for shipment to the United States, and he blamed the Spanish American War for a fall in sales.

The beginning of the end

It was inevitable that the widespread adoption of the motor vehicle would bring about the end of the horse cab. How quickly the change would come was anybody's guess. In Berlin, it was instantaneous, for horse cabs were forbidden by official decree in April 1912. In Britain, it was left to market forces. The tide ran more strongly against horse cabs in London than it did in the provinces. The first electric cabs in London were introduced in 1897. The earliest licence awarded to a petrol-engined cab was in the following year, although motor cabs did not become a permanent feature of the streets until 1903. Before 1907, London had fewer than one hundred motor cabs in operation; by 1910, their number exceeded that of horse cabs. In 1914, when the Metropolitan Police licensed 1391 horse cabs, 7260 motor cabs were approved for public use. In the provinces the changeover was slower, although numbers were much smaller. By 1912, Dublin still had 1333 horse cabs, more than eleven times the number of its motor cabs. Of ten major British provincial cities surveyed in that year, only in Bristol (where motor cabs outnumbered horse cabs by five to one) and Liverpool had the horse cab been ousted from supremacy.

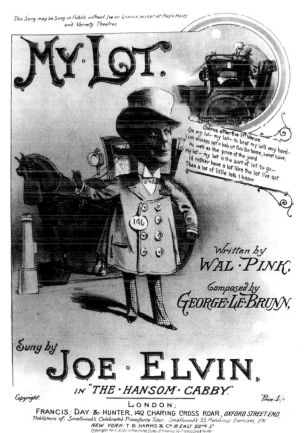

The horse cab was the subject of numerous music-hall songs. This one, dating from about 1900, extols the virtues of the hansom cabby's 'lot' or vehicle and contrasts it with the motor cab, which 'rattle[s] like a cattle truck, and smell[s] like some oil van'.

Between 1903 and 1905 a Royal Commission on London Traffic examined the transport problems of the metropolis. This picture of Piccadilly Circus was submitted in evidence by Sir Alexander Bruce, the Assistant Commissioner of the Metropolitan Police. Omnibuses and hansom cabs constitute the majority of the vehicles to be seen. The horse remains triumphant – although its days were now numbered.

At the Science Museum repository at Wroughton, Wiltshire, a 1910 Renault motor cab is flanked by the kind of vehicle it helped to oust. To its left is a growler, built by Ricketts, and reputed to be one of the first cabs operated by Thomas Tilling in 1864. On the right is an early twentieth-century hansom cab, added to the collection in 1939. The hansom was recognised to be approaching extinction as early as 1912, when one was presented to the museum.

The coming of the motor cab provided an unprecedented opportunity to introduce the taximeter, a device which had been around, in one form or another, since the 1820s, but which had never caught on with horse cabs. In London the Home Office proved remarkably pro-active, and taximeters became standard on motor cabs almost from the start. Their introduction added greatly to the work of the Public Carriage Office, which had to test each meter as well as keep track of it. As meters failed and were repaired, each had to be retested and might be fitted to a new

Devices to measure the distance travelled by a vehicle had been constructed in ancient China, and throughout the nineteenth century enthusiastic inventors offered such machines to the cab-licensing authorities. One such was Von Uster's Patent Mile-Index, shown here in an engraving from the 'Illustrated London News' of 6th February 1847. Before the 1890s, however, none was found suitable, either because of an inability to cope with complicated fare structures, or because they offered little protection against tampering.

Left: 'Humming Birds' is what cab drivers came to call the Bersey electric cab, introduced to London in 1897. Like many early motor cabs, the design was heavily influenced by that of the horse cabs which preceded them.

Below: The early motor-cab driver was only slightly better protected from the elements than the horse-cab driver. Such was the conservatism of the Metropolitan Police that in London a full windscreen on taxicabs was not allowed until 1954. This illustration of the popular Unic cab comes from 'Motor Traction for Business Purposes', published in 1913.

vehicle, all of which had to be recorded. Furthermore, there was the task of testing the motor-handling skills of would-be drivers, once they had passed 'the knowledge'. Horse-cab drivers could proceed immediately to a motor-driving test, which placed them at an advantage, and it was estimated in 1911 that 67 per cent of taxi-cab drivers in London were former horse-cab drivers. Older men found it more difficult to make the transition, partly because employers faced greater difficulties in securing insurance cover for them. In 1910, the drivers' union complained that large numbers of such men were 'gradually being squeezed out into the workhouse'.

Horse cabs did survive the First World War and in 1923 (the centenary year of the London cab) 347 still plied the streets of the metropolis. Even after the last ones disappeared, however, their memory lingered on, partly in the way the hackney cab trade was organised, but particularly in the reputation of the sharp-witted driver.

St. Ann's Square, Manchester.

Left and below: *Two postcards of the cab rank in St Ann's Square, Manchester. The earlier card (below) dates from around 1902. Within twenty years, although there is still horse-drawn traffic on the roads, the motor cab has completely ousted the horse cab.*

Below: *Four-legged and two-legged beneficiaries of the Horses' and Drivers' Aid Committee. The title of the society, formed in 1912, reflects its priorities: the horse came before the man. The society did not aim to retrain drivers – indeed quite the reverse. It set out to equip and provide superior jobbing carriages, 'thus affording employment to cab-drivers who may be too old to learn to drive motors, but not incapable of driving horse-drawn cabs.'*

The last of many – a growler between the wars. From 11,547 in 1898, the number of horse cabs in London had fallen to sixty-nine by 1930. No more were licensed after 1943.

Further reading

Barker, T.C., and Robbins, M. *A History of London Transport*. George Allen & Unwin, volume 1, 1963; volume 2, 1974.

Georgano, G.N. *A History of the London Taxicab*. David & Charles, 1972.

Georgano, Nick. *The London Taxi*. Shire, 1985.

Gilbey, Sir Walter. *Modern Carriages*. Vinton, 1905.

Gordon, W.J. *The Horse World of London*. Religious Tract Society, 1893; reprinted, David & Charles, 1971.

Huggett, Frank E. *Carriages at Eight*. Lutterworth Press, 1979.

McCausland, Hugh. *The English Carriage*. Batchworth Press, 1948.

May, Trevor. *Gondolas and Growlers. The History of the London Horse Cab*. Alan Sutton, 1995.

Moore, H.C. *Omnibuses and Cabs*. Chapman & Hall, 1902.

Sekon, G.A. *Locomotion in Victorian London*. Oxford University Press, 1938.

Smith, D.J. *Discovering Horse-Drawn Vehicles*. Shire, 1994.

Thompson, John. *Horse-Drawn Carriages*. Thompson, 1980.

Waldron, Sallie. *Looking at Carriages*. Pelham Books, 1980.

Two hansoms and a motor cab 'rank it' alongside Decimus Burton's Hyde Park screen. The number of motor cabs licensed in London increased between 1906 and 1908 from 96 to 2805.

A cab stand outside the Brompton Oratory, London, at the turn of the twentieth century (left). The cab shelter at this stand was built in 1897 and still exists in good condition (right). The fretwork panels contain the initials CSF, standing for the Cabmen's Shelter Fund.

Places to visit

The following museums have horse cabs in their collections, although some are private vehicles, never used as hackney carriages.

Abbey Pumping Station Museum, Corporation Road, Abbey Lane, Leicester LE4 5PX.
   Telephone: 0116 299 5111. Website: www.leicestermuseums.ac.uk
Arlington Court, Arlington, Barnstaple, North Devon EX31 4LP. Telephone: 01271 850296.
Bourne Hall Museum, Spring Street, Ewell, Surrey KT17 1UF. Telephone: 0208 3941734.
   Website: www.epsom.townpage.co.uk
Gunnersbury Park Museum, Gunnersbury Park, London W3 8LQ. Telephone: 0208 9921612.
Hinckley Hackney Carriage Museum, A5 Watling Street, Hinckley, Leicestershire LE10 3JA.
   Telephone: 0145 238141. (The collection is housed by the lake next to the hotel. Enquiries should be made to Hinckley and Bosworth Borough Council and not to the hotel.)
Hull Transport Museum, High Street, Hull HU1 1NQ. Telephone: 01482 613902.
   Website: www.hullcc.gov.uk/museums
Maidstone Carriage Museum, Archbishop's Stables, Mill Street, Maidstone, Kent.
   Telephone: 01622 602855. Closed for winter. Open May 1 to August 30.
   Website: www.museum.maidstone.gov.uk
Museum of London, London Wall, London EC2Y 5HN. Telephone: 0207 0019844.
   Website: www.museumoflondon.org.uk
Red House Stables Carriage Museum, Old Road, Darley Dale, Matlock, Derbyshire DE4 2ER.
   Telephone: 01629 733583. Website: www.workingcarriages.com
The Science Museum, D4 Admin Office, Wroughton Airfield, Swindon, Wiltshire SN4 9LT.
   Telephone: 01793 846200. Website: www.sciencemuseum.org.uk/wroughton
Stockwood Craft Museum and Gardens and Mossman Collection, Stockwood Park, Farley Hill, Luton,
   Bedfordshire LU1 4BH. Telephone: 01582 738714.
Worcester County Museum, Hartlebury Castle, Hartlebury, near Kidderminster, Worcestershire
   DY11 7XZ. Telephone: 01299 250416.
York Castle Museum, Eye of York, York YO1 9RY. Telephone: 01904 687687.
   Website: www.yorkcastlemuseum.org.uk

   Twelve Victorian and Edwardian cab shelters are listed as being of architectural and historical importance. In London, they can be found in: Russell Square, WC1; Tavistock Street, WC2; Hanover Square, W1; Warwick Avenue, W9; Kensington Park Road, W11; St George's Square, SW1; Thurloe Place, SW7; and Kensington Road, SW7. Two are in Yorkshire, in Station Road, York, and at Embsay Station. Leicester has one at Humberstone Gate. Ipswich has a former shelter in Bolton Lane. In addition to these listed shelters, a number of others are known to survive.